Connoisseur
of TIME

AN INVITATION TO PRESENCE

**REIMAGINE YOUR RELATIONSHIP
WITH TIME FOR YOUR WELL-BEING**

Joel B. Bennett, PhD

Foreword by Dr. Roger Jahnke, OMD

Preview of the QUEST FOR PRESENCE Collection

ORGANIZATIONAL WELLNESS AND LEARNING SYSTEMS

QUEST FOR PRESENCE MANDALA

The Radiant Forces

Form   Chaos   Nurturing Conditions   Time Shaping

The Soulful Capacities

Acceptance   Presence   Flow   Synchronicity

The Attractions

Crafting   Potentiating   Discerning   Centering   Synthesizing   Coordinating   Intending   Catalyzing   Openir

The Trajectories

Transcendence	————		————	Interruption
Rhythm	————		————	Pacing
Timing	————		————	Routine
Transition	————		————	Scheduling

The Treasures

Start here and flow clockwise

← Spontaneity → Momentousness → Fulfillment → Clutch →
Optimism → Effortlessness → Ordinariness → Coherence →
Adoration → Resonance → Patience → Preciousness →
Savoring → Poignance → Release → Awe → Spontaneity →

Published by

Organizational Wellness and Learning Systems
FLOWER MOUND, TX

ISBNs: 978-0-9915102-6-9 (print) • 978-0-9915102-7-6 (ebook)

This book is not intended as medical or psychological advice. Please consult with a licensed professional if you have questions or concerns. This book represents my own opinions.

The ebook version of this book contains exercises or self-assessments that are best completed by writing or marking statements. You can find downloadable versions of these exercises at www.PresenceQuest.life, the website for the Quest for Presence collection.

The contents and exercises in this book are provided for personal education and learning and should not be interpreted or understood to represent therapeutic or professional advice. Readers are encouraged to seek help from licensed counselors, therapists, or spiritual advisors. This book represents my own personal opinions.

Scripture quotations marked (NIV) are taken from the Holy Bible, New International Version®, NIV®. Copyright © 1973, 1978, 1984, 2011 by Biblica, Inc.™ Used by permission of Zondervan. All rights reserved worldwide. www.zondervan.com. The "NIV" and "New International Version" are trademarks registered in the United States Patent and Trademark Office by Biblica, Inc.™

All quotes are from *A Course in Miracles,* copyright ©1992, 1999, 2007 by the Foundation for Inner Peace, publisher and copyright holder, www.acim.org used with permission.

Editing by Candace Johnson, Change It Up Editing, Inc.; and Sandra Wendel, Write On, Inc.

Cover & interior by Gary A. Rosenberg • www.thebookcouple.com
Mandala art by author, Jeffrey McQuirk, and Rob Supan

Dedicated to my wife Jan,
and to other treasures that turn this
tiniest house of time into a home:

Nora, Emily, Tenzin, Eli,
Isaac, and Cameron

Quest for Presence Collection

Contents

PART 3: TOUCH POINTS

Foreword

That we can re-imagine time as a healthy resource is a secret to longevity, vitality, healing, and power. Re-vision your relationship with time, open a portal to an alternative destiny, and contribute to the sustainability of humanity.

Fortunately, time is mutable. If time can be re-shaped, why not create a version that promotes well-being? By making this clear, my friend Dr. Joel Bennett contributes to your well-being and provides a map for proceeding. Yes, time can take on all kinds of forms. This ancient truth, taught by healers and shamans for thousands of years, has now become the territory of modern wizards: the quantum physicists.

Our contemporary world—governed primarily by only clock-time—can make you feel like there is never enough of it. And yet, the ancient and modern wizards tell us that time is an illusion.

Productivity and time management gurus will tell you, "Time is a matter of priorities ... discover what is meaningful and important to you, and all will be well." This is a subtle form of snake oil because it is still just the same old clock-time done up in a differ-ent dress. We decide what's important based on priori-tizing schedules, blocks of time, or to-do lists. We can only get so far with priorities when all we are prioritizing is a mechanical, linear, and outdated view of time.

You might wonder, "How did those who came long before us survive without strip malls, online shopping, television, the internet, and so forth?" The simple and profound answer is they had more time, at least a more organic, celestial, and mysterious view of time. They didn't work for a boss within a hierarchy of control that required carrying a device to coordinate one's day with the massive machinery of the commercial, industrial complexes. Instead, they contemplated nature's rhythms and celestial influences and celebrated celestial time—sun solstices and equinoxes, the moon full, new, ever changing. The idea of a work day or work week was unnecessary.

You might argue, "Well, we cannot go backward to those uncivilized times when the elements were harsh at times and life was—according to our current assumptions—a struggle." On the one hand, I agree. On the other hand, our current approach is destructive of our essential selves and our well-being. Worse than that, unless "the average person" wakes up to the oppressive and even destructive nature of clock-time, we will continue to prioritize (mostly unconsciously) convenience. We are at risk as we fail to delay gratification and opt for the quick fix. Our planet is less and less habitable. The alarm is blaring—it is now actually dangerous to hit "snooze."

We each have the opportunity to explore a new model of time. I believe that the one offered here by Joel is rich and beautiful enough to support real transformation for you. The quest for presence can be practiced. It can be enjoyed in community. It can take us into contemplative and spiritual arts and practices. Here, we might regain a deeper awareness of our presence to ourselves, to each other, and to this spinning planet as it spirals along through the multiverse.

Indeed, advances in civilization are often characterized by three types of art—the healing, the contemplative, and the practical. All three grow and enrich our lives through presence. All require the skills of pausing, showing up, and listening.

Fortunately, the new model of time introduced in Joel's *The Connoisseur of Time* is a gentle invitation—practical, healing, and contemplative. The quest for presence may be pivotal to how you live your life moving forward. Yes, practice and discipline may be required. But then, we are becoming more purposeful now—more prepared—to tolerate the complexity and even thrive!

You are invited to take a simple first step: make the time to read Joel's short and powerful book. Rearrange your priorities. Give it some time. Discover a new way of relating to time. Your redefined personal view of time will transform your life trajectory and enhance your health span. Take a deep breath. Visualize your preferred self, then emerge with great efficacy as a connoisseur of time... a practitioner of presencing!

Dr. Roger Jahnke, OMD
Author, Trainer, Physician, Founder, The Healer Within Foundation, Institute of Integral Qigong and Tai Chi

The Connoisseur of Time

Over the past several decades of my life, I have delivered hundreds of training programs designed to prevent addiction amongst adult workers. While addiction is one of the greatest barriers to being present to life, I have gleaned deep insights about life from talking to people in recovery from their past obsessions. That includes recovering from my own work addiction or workaholism.

A friend of mine, who used to bartend, recently described the difference between a connoisseur of alcohol—wine, in particular—and an alcoholic or binge drinker. The connoisseur always takes more time, while the alcoholic drinks as though time is running out. Such time compression is universal in all types of addiction and any unhealthy routine of consumption. We want what we want and we want it now while the actual NOW secretly escapes us.

Pausing, slowing down, and taking time with the moment (today, this day) provide effective answers to addiction and most problems with stress, burn-out, and many mental health concerns. Fortunately, anyone can learn these skills. Anyone can be a connoisseur of time.

Your Time and Well-Being: An Invitation

You are invited to pause. And by pause, I mean to create a space in your time (or time in your space), to step outside your normal flow to experience time as a source of well-being. To pause is actually to quest, to go within. It is not too much of a stretch to suggest that our health and well-being—personally and for all of humanity—may depend on being able to pause. Unless we pause, our well-being—personally, in our families, workplaces, and also as a planet—will suffer.

Many barriers to well-being are caused by the felt lack of time or the conventional perception that there is just not enough of it. Here is a list of some of the well-documented symptoms from time pressure:

+ Stress, exhaustion, burnout, poor health, heart disease.

+ Loneliness, alienation, and even depression. These stem from a fast-paced work environment that often includes an unfriendly and even hostile work climate.

- Lack of nutrients that can promote longer and healthier time for digestion and absorption into the body. These are lacking because of fast or processed and ultra-processed foods that also promote time pressure to consume food.

- Less time on weekends or during "off days" for our bodies and minds to unwind and recover.

- Damaged relationships because of rapid-fire and bite-size social media posts (examples are mindless tweets or senseless criticisms).

- Decreased thoughtfulness or critical thinking. We are more likely to believe false information—and experience negative emotions—when under time pressure to consume data (scrolling through social media posts) than when we take the time to deliberate about information.

Research shows that we can avoid these problems and cultivate an ongoing lifestyle that actually removes these problems from our personal lives. Here are three well-documented benefits from a healthy relationship to time:

- Those among us who have well-being are more likely to have set priorities for how they wish to spend their time.

- Those who make time for self-care, leisure, or contemplation tend to experience greater well-being.

✦ Those who have a more expanded and proactive view of time tend to enjoy greater health, well-being, and success in life.

All of these three are reasons for having some motivation, if not curiosity, to take a pause—and thus accept my invitation to begin this quest.

* * *

I want to make this invitation as inclusive as possible, for all people and at any time.

The human experience of transcendence—of something that outlasts us, our sense of timelessness or eternity—is universal, a topic treated by spiritual and religious teachers as well as philosophers, scientists, and atheists. So, I hope you find something here that works for you.

Also, this collection of books is not titled *The Quest for Presence*, suggesting only one way and disrespectful to your own unique time genius. Nor is this simply *A Quest*, implying a singular day-trip or minor excursion. Rather, I use the active, directive (and perhaps commanding) verb "Quest" for Presence. Imagine the connoisseur who encourages you: "You must try this. Taste this. Listen to this. Look at this." Similarly, this is an invitation to start now, jump right in to THIS: your ongoing, and both ordinary and extraordinary, relationship with time … your very unique happening life.

The Ferry Ride

For almost thirty years, my wife and I have vacationed at Crystal Beach on the Bolivar Peninsula in Texas. The last and often the best part of the journey is the twenty-minute ferry from Galveston. We always get out of the car to watch for dolphins. If we pass at the right time, we see them leap high in the air from the bow wave of a giant tanker or container ship. They emerge suddenly and unpredictably in pas de deux, playful pods, and sometimes solo. Right there! A dolphin smiling right at me!

We started these trips long before there were cameras in our phones. I remember children, families and young lovers oohing and aahing as they caught the spontaneous beauty and wonder of a leaping dolphin. Often, they would turn to us, smile, and share in their next spotting:

> *"Did you see that one?"*
> *"Wow! Look at that!"*

Nowadays, however, our fellow ferry-goers lift their phones and scurry to frame the moment when a dolphin or pod emerges. They almost always miss the sighting while fumbling with technology. I have had this experience as well. What's missing I believe (and I also hear more and more often from my clients and students) are the real treasures of light: The experience of Right there! A dolphin smiling right at me!

Why struggle to capture the moment when I can be in the moment?

This is a book about deeply coming to know, appreciate, and making more of time. By "more," I mean by making a bigger deal of time consciously because time is the most important thing we have and don't have. A dolphin encounter may last a moment, and yet there is a wonderful cadence, rhythm, and arc every time a dolphin appears. To fully experience that moment is to literally reset the brain to joy and other treasures you will soon learn about on this journey.

Let's return to the ferry ride so I can explain more.

Many times, we don't see any dolphins. I cultivate patience while scanning the waves. On rare occasions, calculating their cadence just right, I am rewarded because I just know when they will pop up next. Always, however, the ferry pulls into the dock. I look back along the wake as the engine slows; something else gets me every time: It's over. That went by too quickly. There's a tinge of longing. But also savoring. There, in the next moment, ordinary seagulls and pelicans, sentries just waiting for our arrival.

So, this book is also about exploring the idea that timing can bring us many of life's treasures, amongst them ordinariness and poignance as well as awe. Because, mostly, just being present is everything. This book, and others in this collection, provide a set of tools to improve your relationship to time. We need a new language, a map, to help our questing for presence in this happening called life.

PART 1:
PRESENCE

To get started, you are invited to pause, show up, and listen.

Pause

This book concerns the evolution of consciousness in yourself and within humanity. Current crises include war, climate change, political unrest, social alienation, racial injustice, deforestation, pollution, uncontrollable disease and pandemics, population growth, corporate greed, and problems with despair, depression, and anxiety. To face these issues squarely and with any hope of addressing them, it will help to pause.

How did our world get this way?

Based on my research, many of these problems are caused by being imprisoned by a limiting, linear, and mechanistic view of time. This means seeing—and buying and selling—time as only the numerical and ceaseless progression of the clock, the calendar, or other devices.

At one level, climate change is humanity's wake-up call to revise this conventional and limited view of time. The deepest root and natural organic flow of time come from our orientation to the earth in its cyclic aligning to the sun. Mess with that root, and nature calls for a self-correction. Native Americans and indigenous peoples know this basic truth.

The most recent coronavirus pandemic—a direct outgrowth of our messing around—highlighted a preexisting and nearly universal trend among employees. That is: People want more of their own time back, to spend their time on things that bring them meaning, purpose, and joy. They want to be present to their lives.

Corporate America calls this flight from work *The Great Resignation*. This label reveals a self-serving or egocentric perspective. This viewpoint started with the industrialization of work and the rise of employers as attempted masters of our personal and private time. Our desire to take back our time is intimately related to climate change. We know the well-oiled treadmill of economy can only help us evolve so far.

Our time has been broken: commercialized, commoditized, capitalized, corporatized, and computerized, accompanied by an excessive craving for speed, the rise of the 24/7 society, techno-invasion, and a push-button stupor. In just the past generation, we have seen the steady deterioration of those sacred days once set aside weekly for spiritual contemplation. Perhaps it will help to pause or, if you are a workaholic, completely stop.

Show Up

Imagine you are a connoisseur who has seen, heard, or tasted something new and powerfully irresistible. You might just simply treasure the moment. Alternatively, you might be spurred to embark on an adventure—a quest—to understand where this new discovery came from. What ingredients were used? Where were they sourced? Who grew, created, or designed this wonder?

There are three ways to approach being a connoisseur:

1. one who seeks to enjoy, appreciate, and discriminate subtleties;

2. one who wants to understand the details, technique, or principles of an art and then help others; and

3. one who *takes the time* to explore the background, the history, or the origin and diverse processes and people behind the taste, the hue, the musical note.

These three approaches roughly correspond to being a seeker, a practitioner, and a scholar. This book, and the Quest for Presence collection, offer exercises for all three. All invite you to show up to life, and grow in wisdom about the treasures that await you there. So, show up in any way that works for you.

Let's reflect on my ferry-ride adventures. Over several few years, I have collected dozens of similar "treasure" stories from students and friends. My story—and all others I have collected—are not only about wonder. Dolphin-sighting is not the only treasure. Those ordinary, dirty seagulls are also part of the whole collage. Presence also reveals poignance, patience, effortlessness, optimism, and letting go. The time connoisseur notices dozens of flavors (sweet and sour) and hues (light and shadow).

Again, anyone can be a connoisseur. You might enjoy the bubbles as you are washing the dishes, the aroma of coffee, the crackling autumn leaves beneath your feet, or just sitting with a child. But you might go further. As a metaphor, consider the connoisseur of exotic teas who travels to tea farms and tea gardens to witness how the tea is grown, harvested, and crafted. They might speak to the locals, find a family who has worked in a tea garden for generations, and even become an apprentice.

I am not suggesting that everyone need or should make these extra efforts. However, due to the chronic health issues linked to the pressures of clock-time and time compression, the entire Quest for Presence collection offers readers a new language and detailed map for exploring … just in case. For now, I want to meet you wherever you are in your own quest.

I likely don't know what led you to read this book

or whether you will want to dig deeper. You may be free from or held captive by work and the need to succeed. You may be bouncing back from trauma or relaxing on a beautiful day. A friend, coach, or therapist may have suggested this book or provided it as a gift.

Wherever you are, my job is to hold you for a moment. I want these words to hug you just long enough so that you can revitalize—even revolutionize— your relationship with time, allowing you to be fully present in this life you have been given. Two scenarios may help. First, imagine that you read this to a loved one who is close to death and only has a few days left of mental clarity. Second, perhaps you just returned from the funeral of a loved one or experienced other significant loss.

Both of these seemingly extreme circumstances call us to be present. I refer to these as *seemingly* extreme circumstances because for many who come to this quest, an inkling arises; namely, as human beings we wake up to our extraordinary situation. This is it! Life is happening. We are happening to life. Our time here is limited. We can (we must) choose to better show up in whatever way we can.

Listen

Rather than organize your life in units of conventional time (days, hours, minutes), perhaps organize it in transformational units of value and personal meaning. I would like you to do an exercise, actually, the first of several exercises. This should take less than ten minutes of your clock-time.

Here are twenty different statements. Before reading them, reflect on your attitude toward time, time management, how you spend your time, and how much you schedule your time around important priorities. Also, notice how you feel in your body when you reflect on your attitude toward time. In short, have you grasped just how limited your time is in this life? Have you given that concept enough thought?

This exercise may help you decide if this quest is right for you *at this time*. The decision to move in a new direction should not be taken lightly. Consider you are about to embark on a life-changing journey. Reimagining time as a source of well-being may be a momentous decision.

STEP 1. Note Your Experience. Read each statement. Note on a separate piece of paper or place a checkmark on the worksheet you can download from my website (www.PresenceQuest.life). Note any statement you have ever experienced that you can recall. Wait for further instructions after making any checkmarks. If none are familiar, then check the one that most resonates with you or that you agree with.

1. *We are all going to die anyway; why bother setting aside time?*

2. *I am in a really bad place and don't have time to think about it.*

3. *My life is a numbing routine or treadmill.*

4. *I never have enough time to do what I want.*

5. *I am too busy, impatient, or pressed to get things done.*

6. *I struggle to find time for things that matter.*

7. *With so many competing priorities, I often don't have time for myself.*

8. *When I get home from work, I don't have the time for things that bring me joy.*

9. *My time is spent helping other people, not myself.*

10. *My efforts at managing time are not very effective.*

11. *My efforts at managing time have brought me some well-being.*

12. *I can readily deepen my awareness of the moment.*

13. *My body feels open and calm because of my relationship with time.*

14. *I have all the time I need for life, work, leisure, and more.*

15. *My life is one unfolding project of pattern and meaning.*

16. *I accept what is, am present to my life, flow with change, and find meaningful patterns in my life.*

17. *I am attracted to the unfolding and fulfillment of my destiny.*

18. *My expansive view of time includes embracing forces in the universe, my past and future self, and the fullness of my day.*

19. *My day is filled with treasures, day-to-day, every day.*

20. *I am aware of and attracted to timeless and eternal qualities; my truest identity is ultimately beyond time.*

STEP 2. Note Your Feelings. Now that you have completed reviewing your statements, look again at each one you noted, especially those that stood out for you or that you most resonated with. Please select only one or two. Reflect on the feelings, emotional tone, or mood the statement(s) evokes in you. Breathe. Bring attention to how you feel in your body. Please write down those feelings. In case you have difficulty, consult the following list. These are examples, so it may help to use these only as prompts for finding the best label for your feeling or body sensation.

Bored	Helpless	Yearning	Curious
Anxious	Understanding	Attached	Peaceful
Excitement	Connection	Warmth	Meaning
Joyful	Uplifted	Optimistic	Sensitive
Hurt	Grace	Easy	Stuck
Insecure	Torn	Restless	Waking
Guilty	Overwhelmed	Expansive	Restricted
Effortless	Apathetic	Spontaneous	Preciousness
Open	Struggling	Amazed	Accepting

STEP 3. Identify Your Common Tendency. This next step requires being fully present and honest with yourself—where do you hang out most of the time? What is your most common tendency? Which one of the twenty statements in step 1 best describe your general attitude toward the time you are using in your life? Okay, okay, you might be thinking that you cannot just choose only one. Feel free to select a few but no more than two. Copy that same sentence (or sentences) on a separate piece of paper or on the worksheet. If you notice any feelings (positive or negative) just be with them for a moment and, when ready, go to Step 4.

STEP 4. Identify The Threshold. Go back and note a single statement (and associated feelings) that you would like to experience more often. For this exercise, we will call this *The Threshold* statement and feelings. Now contemplate—or take a moment to reflect on— why you selected the threshold statement or what it all means to you. Where are you now in your life? Where are you headed? What is attracting you to a new or more common attitude? What feelings would you like to experience more of?

STEP 5. Be Aware of Gaps. Take note of both your common tendency statements (step 3) and The Threshold statement and feelings (step 4). Just pause for a moment and take a deep breath as you review them both. Based on the instructions, there is likely some gap between where you are currently and where you would like to go.

Suggestion: Write down both your common tendency and your threshold statement together. Keep these with you. Look at them for a few days and just notice what comes up. Your decision to continue on this journey will depend on this gap and any feelings, tension, desire, or need you have in response to this gap. We will return to the important idea of The Threshold later. But first, let's make sure this quest is for you.

Embark?

L et's assume you have now paused, shown up, and listened. Do you want or need to travel further?

There are six reasons why you may choose not to read further, step up to The Threshold, or take that first step on your quest. There are also five reasons why this process or journey may be exactly what you need.

Possible Reasons for Staying Put, Waiting, Not Reading Further

1. **Inertia.** Your common tendency from step 3 was checking only the first one or two statements. For example, the first statement: *We are all going to die anyway; why bother setting aside time?* If you identify with this and only this, then I think you may lack the effort and energy required for the journey. No worries. You can always come back later. I actually started out at this place many years ago. It was only because I stepped up to The Threshold that I came to experience all the other statements. So, I encourage you to keep reading. However, if you are also feeling depressed or have suicidal thoughts, I hope you will reach out for help (please check out https://988lifeline.org/ or dial 988).

2. **You are already there.** Also, here is the last statement: *I am aware of and attracted to timeless and eternal qualities; my truest identity is ultimately beyond time.* If you identify with this and only this, then I think you have, as it were, arrived. You have transcended and fulfilled, and your understanding of time is complete. In other words, you have completed the journey, and you don't need to read my book.

3. **You really are just too busy.** You might be a single parent or at a stage in your career, education, or life where you are already full-throttle into this happening life. You don't have time. You have other priorities. You trust that things will sort themselves out. If so, you may already have started the quest, and taking time to reflect may not serve you right now.

4. **There is no gap; your motivation is low.** You may indeed be exactly where you need to be, and it may be best to just stay there for now. That is perfectly fine and often the best place to be. Why go looking for trouble? If it isn't broken, why fix it?

5. **This all seems just a luxury right now.** This may certainly be true. You may be just getting by, or you have enough to handle with life's routines. Taking time out may be an indulgence that doesn't sit right with you.

6. **You avoid anything spiritual, including New Age philosophy.** If you have read all twenty statements, you likely have the sense that the quest has some

spiritual, philosophical, or transcendental aspects to it; at least these statements suggest as much:

I am attracted to the unfolding and fulfillment of my destiny.

My expansive view of time includes embracing forces in the universe, my past and future self, and the fullness of my day.

You may just not be into spirituality. From the outset, I should have emphasized that questing includes transcendental features. We are only here, in this human body, for a limited time. The expanse of time in our presence journey suggests that we explore beyond the limits of our biology. We might embrace soul, spirit, or an essence beyond our personality. To be clear, we are not advocating a religion or asking you to join a cult. In fact, the next exercise asks you to contemplate statements about time from different texts, both religious and atheist. Still, I completely understand if spirituality is not important right now.

Possible Reasons for Forging Ahead and Reading Further

1. **There is a gap, and you feel motivated.** Something is stirring inside of you to explore notions of time beyond what you have learned from your culture and upbringing. You sense something is not quite right about our fast-paced, 24/7 digital world. You are deeply concerned about the state of humanity, the planet, the climate crisis, and the rise of pandemics.

2. **You are burned out and/or care deeply about your well-being.** You realize the old ways are not working; at least, they have caused you to feel burned out and exhausted. You know you need a new approach to life for more well-being and happiness.

3. **You have reached a limit with time-management tools.** You recognize there is more to managing time than just the goal of efficiency. You want to expand your ideas of what your successful use of time might look like.

4. **You are the curious type and know there is more to life.** You have had an experience that spoke to your dream for more knowledge, a better life, or enlightenment. You may have felt for a while that you need to change your way of living. You may want more joy or insight.

5. **You want more spirituality (spiritual health, self-transcendence).** You have not devoted the time, space, and energy you need to cultivate your relationship with the divine, a higher power, or transcendent principles or virtues. You either want to return to your soul or take the time to get to know it in the first place.

PART 2:
THE QUEST

The word "quest" suggests a search, a move into the future. Here, it means simply being, a settling into the present. Such settling is often a challenge. Fortunately, thousands of insights from philosophy and spiritual and religious texts may help you cross the threshold and embody the treasures of life.

The Threshold

A nything that gets you out of yourself and connects you to something expansive and spacious—that helps you marvel—frees you from time compression. Anyone can have this experience and within everyday life. You do not need superpowers to pause, show up, listen, and embark. In today's world, it would seem that contemplative efforts are heroic. Rest assured. Not all heroes wear capes.

Modern time-heroes wear watches but also know when to take them off and return to the things that matter. They honor clock-time but also reimagine their relationship with time as a source of well-being. They flow with time rather than feel constricted by the hours left in their day.

Often, the most decisive moment in the hero's journey occurs when they set out or are forced to leap into the new, the different, the unknown. Risk, if not all-out danger, lies ahead. No quest, no threshold; and no genuine threshold without a trembling sense of the challenge ahead.

I am a fan of Michael Meade, the poet, storyteller, and teacher of mythic imagination. I recommend his books (for example, *Awakening the Soul*) and his podcast "Living Myth." Michael talks about thresholds, their importance to a well-led life for oneself and the collective soul of humanity. Meade explains:

The idea of a threshold is something that exists before one state and another, before one place and another. Most of us are collectively on that threshold betwixt and between the letting go of the old view of the world and the full stepping into the new world.

We are talking about a "full stepping," throwing oneself into the matter—or most simply, presence. A threshold connects one phase and another. It may show up as a gateway, an initiation, an emergence. We are called to make a decision to go down one path instead of another, to let go of the door and step into the unknown. To stop playing it safe. To follow one's bliss.

Your presence grows to the degree that you live wholeheartedly in the gap between where you are now and what you want. Return to the twenty statements and review Step 4: Identify the Threshold. Remember, this is an exercise. The wording of The Threshold statement may not sit exactly right for you. Only you know what stirs inside, how much pain you have endured to now embark on the new, how curious you are, or how barren your spiritual life has become.

Thresholds involve challenges. I challenge you to explore and move into a new way—of *being in time.* Stop playing around, dallying, or exploring one side road after another. In our modern world, some adults take one course or get one educational certificate after another. Much of this occurs online or virtually. It is not at all clear to me how these pursuits do anything but reinforce the preexisting self.

Perhaps new information is gained, but have people really taken much risk? Each person has to decide for themselves. I am not saying these courses have no value. The question is do they lead us toward being. Either way, you are invited to BE on the threshold as you quest for presence, and embody well-BEing.

Time and Spiritual Health

Those who more effectively use time management are more likely to have higher levels of well-being than those who do not. In 2021, three researchers from Canada published a peer-reviewed synthesis of 158 high-quality studies that together examined the relationship between time management and several outcomes.[*] This meta-analysis of 53,957 individuals showed not only that time management works but also the extent to which it had an impact on performance (in both professional and academic settings), well-being (including job and life satisfaction and positive mental health), and distress (reducing anxiety and both physical and psychological distress).

The major finding of interest for our discussion here was somewhat of a surprise to the researchers. Not only did those with time-management skills have higher well-being, but these skills had a more uniform or consistent relationship with well-being than with

---

[*] Aeon, B., Faber, A., & Panaccio, A. (2021). Does time management work? A meta-analysis. *PLOS ONE*, 16(1), e0245066. https://doi. org/10.1371/journal.pone.0245066. Note. Quotes from this article remove scientific citations and italics are added for emphasis. Also, this reference to recent research is one of hundreds documented in the Quest for Presence collection.

performance. People, as it turns out, may use time management more for life satisfaction than for efficiency. Yes, they are less likely to procrastinate, have higher motivations to study and work, and are more proactive.

> *Your proactive, self-determined, and purposeful orientation to time may be a secret to your well-being.*

Importantly, those who manage their time well also have a higher internal locus of control or self-determination. They are more likely to be the captain of their own ship. The researchers write that the effect of time management on *life* satisfaction is 72 percent stronger than on *job* satisfaction. Considering that time management also brings less stress, boredom, and anxiety, we have to assert that a proactive, self-determined, and purposeful orientation to time may be a secret to well-being.

In their discussion, the Canadian researchers conclude that their findings challenge intuitive ideas concerning what time management is for. They write: "This runs against the popular belief that time management primarily helps people perform better and that well-being is simply a byproduct of better performance" and cite other studies that show time-management interventions increase well-being in the absence of performance gains and also benefit the unemployed.

For ease of presentation, the quoted paragraph that follows removes seven additional research citations, but I encourage you to follow the link (see footnote) to review the original study for its wealth of information.

> *Historically people have managed time for other reasons than efficiency, such as spiritual devotion and philosophical contemplation. It is only with relatively recent events, such as the Industrial Revolution and waves of corporate downsizing, that time management has become synonymous with productivity. We hope future research will widen its scope and look more into outcomes other than performance, such as developing a sense of meaning in life. One of the earliest time management studies, for instance, explored how time management relates to having a sense of purpose. However, very few studies followed suit since. Time management thus stands to become a richer, more inclusive research area by investigating a wider array of outcomes.*

Yes, only recently have we forgotten what our time is for. But as soon as you take a proactive approach (*quest* as a verb), you start threading a needle into a weave that is the narrative of your own destiny. I call this a *precious weave of time,* and it is an ongoing, meaningful, and purposeful shuttling back and forth of the moments, occasions, and events of your life.

What Is Spirituality?

In the previous section, I reported on a rigorous research paper about time management. In their conclusion, the authors happened to reference four hallmarks of most endeavors to embrace the transcendent experiences that life has to offer:

+ *Devotion*

+ *Contemplation*

+ *Sense of meaning*

+ *Sense of purpose*

I don't think it a coincidence that our relationship to time includes (and is perhaps inextricably tied to) our relationship to spirituality. At the same time, I know—from teaching this material dozens of times to both professional and religious audiences—to be extra cautious when defining spirituality. I often return to this quote from Saint Teresa of Ávila (Spanish mystic, 1515–1582):

> *We ought not to insist on everyone following in our footsteps, nor to take upon ourselves to give instructions in spirituality when, perhaps, we do not even know what it is.*

I interpret Saint Teresa to mean that we each can find our own definition. Whether it is essence, inner-most being, soul, or whatever term uplifts or enlivens you. "Wherever we come alive, that is the area in which we are spiritual" (Brother David Steindl-Rast from his book *Music of Silence: A Sacred Journey Through the Hours of the Day*).

Whatever term you use, consider contemplation—or rather, practicing the art of contemplation. Indeed, the word *temp*, meaning time, is found in the words *template*, *temple*, and *contemplation*. When we contemplate, we set aside time to lift our thoughts to matters that transcend time. You need not consider those to be only spiritual matters. All that is important is the intention and practice *of setting aside time*. Temples were built to serve all, if not the most "common" people throughout history as reminders of the heavens, gods, goddesses, God, and the most divine.

A Contemplation

Here is another exercise, actually a template for contemplation. This will take anywhere from fifteen to forty-five minutes to complete. I have facilitated this exercise many times, and I encourage you to practice with others. Take time to journal your response. Lead a discussion. Privately share with friends and family.

This section includes texts from diverse faiths and philosophies, all of which make explicit reference to time. Each offers a unique perspective. Each evokes a different set of feelings. For now, simply read them. You may also choose to settle into a quiet space, remove all distractions, take a moment to breathe deeply, relax, and attain a contemplative mood. Again, take a few minutes to slowly read and reflect on these passages.

After taking time to contemplate, I will ask you to reflect on your feelings about these passages. You will receive very specific reflection questions. Each one is important to journal about. At the end of this exercise, you will be guided to integrate and embody your insights and wisdom. Please note that there is no perfect or right way to experience this contemplation. Whatever comes up for you is fine.

Know that the world will outlive you.
How you live your life will affect others,
whether or not you are around to know it.
You want to be the kind of person
who has the larger view,
who takes other's interests into account,
who's dedicated to principles you can justify
like justice,
knowledge,
truth,
beauty
and morality.

> ~ Adapted from Steven Pinker, cognitive psychologist and atheist (from *A Better Life: 100 Atheists Speak Out on Joy & Meaning in a World without God* by Chris Johnson)

* * *

Show me, O Lord, my life's end
and the number of my days;
let me know how fleeting is my life.

My life is a handbreadth before thee . . .

We are but phantoms going to and fro;
heaping up all kinds of wealth;
never knowing where
it will all go.

~ Psalm of David (Psalms 39:4–6; adapted from NIV)

* * *

Consider the lilies of the field, . . .
they neither toil nor spin,

Yet I tell you, even Solomon in all his glory was
   not arrayed like one of these. . .
Therefore, do not be anxious, saying, "What
   shall we eat?"
or "What shall we drink?" or "What shall
   we wear?" . . .

Do not be anxious about tomorrow, for tomorrow
   will be anxious for itself.
Sufficient for the day is its own trouble.

~ Jesus Christ (Matthew 6:28–34; adapted from ESV)

* * *

Thus, shall ye think of all this
fleeting world . . .

a star at dawn,
a bubble in a stream,
a flash of lightning in a summer cloud,
a flickering lamp,
a phantom,
and a dream.

~ The Buddha (Diamond Sutra)

* * *

I swear by the time
(the evening tide),
Everyone is in a state of loss,
Except those who believe
and do good and
join together in truth,
patience, and constancy.

~The Holy Qur'an (adapted)
  (Chapter 103: Al-Asr; The Eventide)

* * *

"Now" has no meaning to the ego.
Now is the closest approximation of eternity
that this world offers.
It is in the reality of "now,"
without past or future,
that the beginning of the appreciation
of eternity lies…

The holy instant is a miniature of eternity.
It is a picture of timelessness, set in
a frame of time…

The whole of Heaven lies in this instant,
borrowed from eternity and set in time for you.

~From "A Course in Miracles" (Foundation
for Inner Peace); excerpts from "The
Function of Time" and "The Two Pictures."
(ACIM, T-13.IV; T-17.IV)

* * *

There are so many gifts
Still unopened from your birthday,
There are so many hand-crafted presents
That have been sent to you by God.

The Beloved does not mind repeating,
"Everything I have is also yours."

Please forgive Hafiz and the Friend
If we break into a sweet laughter
When your heart complains of being thirsty
When ages ago
Every cell in your soul
Capsized forever
Into this infinite golden sea.

~ Sham-ud-din Muhammad Hafiz (c. 1320–1389)

* * *

STEP 1. First Feelings. How did you feel upon reading these passages (any of them or even just one line of them)? Just write down any feelings you have. Again, go inward and become aware of how you feel in your body.

STEP 2. Feeling Prompts. Here is another list of feelings. These are prompts for you, but always return to your first response if these do not fit. Sometimes, it helps to have these prompts so you can articulate your feelings more accurately. Feel free to review the passages again to explore your feelings even more deeply.

Note: For the following words, please note whether the previous passages either stimulated or evoked the associated feeling or whether they led you to feel a *desire, yearning, or hope* to have more of that feeling in your life. Both of these—actual feeling or a desire for the feeling—are important to recognize for this exercise.

Calm	Sense of Meaning
Yearning	Longing
Just Being	Harmony
Coming Home	Belonging
Luminosity	Absorbed
Being in Tune With	Togetherness
Surrender	Relief
Awe	Wonder
Spontaneity	Humility
Something Momentous	A Waking Up
Patience	Allowing
Preciousness	Affection
Savoring	Delight
Poignance	Forgiveness
Fulfillment	Accomplishment
Strength	Victory
Optimism	Goodness
Transcendence	Opening
Effortlessness	Gratitude

STEP 3. Feelings in Your Life. Review these questions for journaling and for discussion with others.

✦ As you reflect on each of the feelings you have, take a moment to note which phrases or passages helped that feeling come into being. Alternatively, did all of the passages work together to evoke a feeling?

✦ When during your life do you have a sense of these feelings?

- During the week
- During the workday
- Morning or evening
- On the weekend
- At special times
- On special days

STEP 4. Origin. Now that you have had time to reflect, it is important to also consider—or imagine—the origin point of each of the passages.

✦ What prompted each passage to be written?

✦ What was it (feelings and thoughts) that inspired the authors to write them?

✦ To what degree was it some contact with a transcendental idea or spiritual source?

✦ What actually happened to bring about the insight, event, or inspiration?

Embodiment of Treasures

Thank you for completing the previous exercise. The feelings you experienced were sent as treasures. Imagine that the passages were themselves written as a vehicle, a vessel, or a conduit. They were created for you.

Each and every one of these wisdom writings, and many more, were designed with you in mind. The feelings they produced are living gifts inside of you. They do not lie dormant waiting to awaken. Rather, they were sent to you a very long time ago and have also always been with you. The passages were only created to help you receive the messages. The feelings have a divine origin. They exist in a place beyond time. As a human being, you have the equipment and opportunity to notice them. You were called to notice them. They are continually being sent to you.

Use the following affirmations to help you embody this sense of being a part of a larger unfolding. This sense will guide your quest for presence. This sense—the deep inner feeling—is your North Star, your guide point. As you cultivate this sense, any problems you have with time pressure will evaporate. You will become more present to your life.

+ I easily embrace the big picture, knowing the world will outlive me.

+ I am happy to admit that I do not know how it will all turn out.

+ I let go of all anxiety about tomorrow, knowing that tomorrow will take care of itself.

+ I experience all of this as a happy bystander as it all comes and goes.

+ Every day is a gift sent for my awakening to the beauty and preciousness of life.

+ I join others who know all of this in their own quest for presence.

PART 3: TOUCH POINTS

The five books in the Quest for Presence collection are filled with different aphorisms, or wisdom sayings, that may be additional touch points for you as you quest. Here are some to get you started.

The Map,
A Precious Weave of Time

First setting out, we see the journey with a map. But this is an imperfect metaphor. As soon as we dive in, an ongoing precious weave emerges, a dynamic tapestry, a swirling mandala. Our life is not a calendar we hop upon. Threads pushed by life and pulled by death. An ever-widening and deepening loom, made by our actions ... and our just waiting with the ordinary.

We think that excitement and joy in life come from living, but maybe it is the other way around. Yes, the thrill is in the ride, but the ride is also in the thrill.

There are always bridges out from any island of pain. Whenever you feel isolated, stuck, without any sense of connection to your future, always know that there are bridges out of here. The treasure lies in the very fact that you are walking on a bridge.

The capacity for "making it in life" is quite different from the capacity for deeply experiencing, embracing, and appreciating your brief time—your whole life—here.

You are already here; you might as well make the most of it (while it lasts).

Life and nature has great complexity but it is only our lack of presence that makes it so complicated.

The Radiant Forces

Your life itself is an unfolding of beautiful Radiant Forces inviting you to dance, giving you the energy to bop, twirl, or chassé, and playing music all the while in the background. Listen and every occasion becomes a step in that dance. Without presence, you may lose your footing.

Everything in life is a self-regulating process. A living system acts (Time Shapes) to maintain stability (Form) while adjusting to ongoing conditions and perturbations (Chaos) that are optimal for growth and becoming (Nurturing Conditions).

Everything has its own time. There is a waiting time, a growing time, and a coming-into-its-own time. Nurturing Conditions call us to wait, listen, discern, and align.

Everything is moving toward some end-state and—through cause and effect—influencing and being influenced by other activity. Time Shaping calls us to take action, make a decision to select and exhibit one behavior over another.

The contents of your mind are no different from fundamental forces that reside throughout the universe. Every regret or resentment reflects a moment to recognize past conditions that have nurtured life. You are called to honor the wisdom of the past instead of nurturing negativity.

The Soulful Capacities

The capacities are temporal competencies acting like windows into the soul.

With Acceptance, our attention becomes spacious and allowing. With Presence, our focus is more substantive, immediate, and discovering. With Flow, our attention itself proceeds into time, and our sense of time subsides as we interact with the task at hand. With Synchronicity, we are caught off guard, resonating and reverberating. Time takes on the quality of something bigger than ourselves.

Ultimately, you are called to accept what is, be present to the change that is unfolding, Flow with it, and ride the tide of synchronicity that is likely to unfold. This is where many Treasures lie.

Your soul is here to work with and through your personality to help you through life challenges and help you see the Treasures of this life.

The Attractions:
Unfolding and Enfolding

Avoid seeing your personality as something that is fixed, set in stone, an assemblage of traits. Rather, you are evolving no matter your age and at every stage of life. The same dynamic forces that make up the entire universe are also gently pulling at you, smiling all the time and wondering.

In a way, you are building the bridge as you walk on it. Your self is also unfolding (verb) and you are also an unfolding (noun). Time only came to nudge you out a bit, get you to swim about, explore.

Our essence, all the information of who we ever were and who we could ever be, is enfolded within our personality. And our personality is not our essence.

We are all attracted to something—to be better, more whole—and also there are aspects of our self that are unattractive. So, as you move into the future, consider the cautions and challenges but also know what moves you—in career, relationships, and the Treasures.

The Trajectories

There are almost 100 different uses or connotations as well as idioms for the word "time" in the English language. Every day, swimming in this sea of time, we rarely pause to see how we use this language.

When we talk about presence, we refer to a mosaic: features of time that play and dance during your day—pace, rhythm, transition, timing, routine, and schedule. For many, presence often refers to the timing of their day and how they bring attention to time. But sometimes, we are lifted up by the simplest things. Time escapes us entirely.

Remember, everything is always in transition. When you feel stuck in a rut, take time to notice the bigger picture of your life. When you feel imprisoned by your schedule, pause to listen to the rhythm of your day. Pace yourself amidst all the distractions and interruptions. As you do these things, timing will do its magic, everything will fall into place, all will work out in the end.

At the deepest and most basic level of reality, everything is a blur. Sometimes, it helps to just sit with it all. Maybe, stop having to make sense of what is happening. You might be surprised by the Treasures there.

The Treasures

There is a deeper reality to life's treasures. A treasure is an experience where you directly witness the value or preciousness of life as it is happening. You have been gifted with human attention but often get lost in the blur. Still, the treasures are there. You only need to take back your time.

It is not possible to fully affirm life's treasures without also acknowledging both their light and dark sides. Our soul does not only dance with the forces in the light. By viewing and holding the shadow side of our life with compassion and care, the shadow dances to show the treasure with greater clarity.

* * *

As you grow beyond your common tendencies, past The Threshold, you will likely immerse your very being into this fleeting world that outlives you. I hope to join you there. At least know that I, along with many others on this quest, are just being there as well.

You might feel that you need to let go of the past and unhelpful mental states, that there is work to be done, that the planet needs saving, and that you want to capture more Treasures regardless of everything else.

No matter what, in the end, it is your time. I am confident that you will make the very most of it—with your presence.

Quest for Presence: A Preview of the Five Books

By all accounts, time does not exist. It is a very old myth. I wonder, if time doesn't exist at all, then why not create a helpful version? I invite you to consider that our allegiance to clock-time—a single linear progression from past to future—may not be the healthiest perspective to take. And yet here we are: 24/7, always on, treadmill, burn out, workaholism, fast-paced, fast-food, and losing precious time while mindlessly surfing the internet or fiddling with the next best technology.

We could do better. We need a new, much friendlier, interesting, curious, and more comprehensive view of time; one that transcends the incessant mechanics of clock-time and brings us back to our senses. So, this is what I set out to do in five books. Each book helps you see this new vision—a precious weaving, an ongoing kaleidoscope or mandala of time as it unfolds in your life. Each contains exercises (contemplations), self-assessments, poetry, and reference to the latest research.

BOOK 1: The Map and Radiant Forces. Many scientists believe that if time is anything, it is the physicist's *arrow of time*. The gradual and chaotic disintegration of everything—the direction physicists call entropy—is always in the background; we know we are going to die someday. Entropy is only one of four fundamental, cosmic, and Radiant Forces. There is also gravity (the incessant drawing together of things); causality or karma (actions matter—we influence what comes next; we reap what we sow); and nurturing conditions (you would not be here if events—billions of nanoseconds—had not previously conspired to bring you into existence).

Book 1 is devoted to helping you understand how these forces work and also dance together; a precious weave of energy that brings about your most intimate experience of your own happening life as existing in the *whole time* of your life.

BOOK 2: The Soulful Capacities. The Radiant Forces appear metaphysical and exist throughout everything, so they seem hard to grasp. However, you as a unique human being have a deep capacity to experience them and fully embrace the whole time of your life. Actually, you have four Soulful Capacities. These are acceptance, presence, flow, and synchronicity. In my studies, it seems that every spiritual path or religious teaching touches on these capacities and usually all of them. We make the most of our time here (and glimpse our role in the universe) when we accept what is, show up fully and present to life, flow

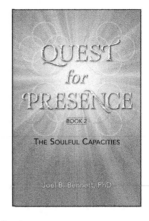

with events and challenges, and glimpse moments—perhaps all moments—as wonderful coincidences that were meant to happen, with purpose, and with meaning.

Book 2 offers many contemplations and introduces a self-assessment tool (the Quest for Presence Inventory™ or QFPI™), designed to help you understand and cultivate these soulful capacities.

BOOK 3: The Attractions. The Radiant Forces are calling you to live out your destiny. At the most soulful level, your time in this life is an unfolding of events that are attracting you toward some fulfillment. In a sense, you are attracted to the Radiant Forces or, more specifically, to a unique combination of them.

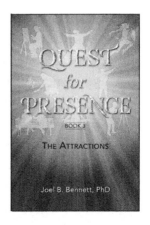

Book 3 presents an alternative view of personality that avoids labeling you as a particular type. Instead, you are typically *in some process* of attracting certain situations to you which, over time, bring insight into your destiny. I identify nine attractions: crafting, potentiating, discerning, centering, synthesizing, coordinating, intending, catalyzing, and opening. The second part of the QFPI helps you assess which of these is currently most active in your life.

BOOK 4: The Trajectories. You may wonder about more mundane aspects of your experience of time in your day-to-day or week-to-week aspects of your life. The Radiant Forces not only influence and guide your personality and self-development (see Book 3), they also influence how eight different  aspects of time show up in your life. In other words, the Radiant Forces dance with each other to produce our experience of first, these seven trajectories: routine, scheduling, transition, timing, rhythm, interruption, and pacing. They also bring about our experience of time transcendence altogether. In other words, we come back to the reality that time is an illusion because we have moments in our lives—in the very midst of our lives—where we experience timelessness or a sense of something eternal, impermanent, precious, or so exquisitely ordinary that we know there is so much more to this happening life than clock-time.

Book 4 showcases each trajectory through poetry, art, exercises, and essays that integrate research and previous scholarly writings. You also have a Day Crafting™ Tool so you can track your experience of the Trajectories over time.

BOOK 5: The Treasures. Life is amazing and so much more colorful, dynamic, and engaging compared to the clock-work universe. All the previous features of our mandala engage in different types of dances (tangos and fandangos, jitterbugs and waltzes) together—the Radiant Forces, the Soulful

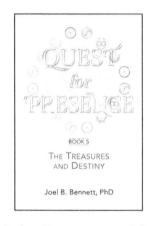

Capacities, the Attractions, and the Trajectories. Of all these, the dance between each of the four Radiant Forces and the four Soulful Capacities gives birth to moments of experiencing life as a true treasure.

Book 5—through poetry and contemplations—unpacks the four-by-four grid and helps you to glimpse the sixteen Treasures that are waiting for you. These are spontaneity, momentousness, fulfillment, clutch, optimism, effortlessness, ordinariness, coherence, adoration, resonance, patience, preciousness, savoring, poignance, release, and awe. You also receive a worksheet to help you identify the light and shadow of each Treasure.

* * *

Overall, there are over fifty contemplations across all five books, and there is also a companion workbook for personal and group work. All of the books, the contemplations, tools, and workbook are designed to help you cultivate a new knowledge of time. This is a process we call *Tempognosis™*, defined as the process of having knowledge (gnosis) of time (temp) in our own personal life and for nurturing the journey of our soul in this life. Contemplations are a method for practicing Tempognosis.

When we contemplate, we become conscious of our soul. The experience of any Treasure is proof that we are engaging in Tempognosis. We remember that the Treasures—as a function of our Soulful Capacities and the Radiant Forces—are always available to us because our soul and the Radiant Forces are always and ever here for our entire lives.

A Bonus Contemplation

The following chart helps you to put many attitudes toward time in context. No matter "when" you are, you always have the opportunity to make time your friend. Where and when are you today? Where and when do you want to go next? Use the chart as a time connoisseur's guide.

TEMPOGNOSIS	*My day is filled with treasures (and through all below)*
TIME WISDOM (THE TREASURES)	*My expansive view of time includes Radiant Forces, my past and future self, and the fullness of my day.*
TIME GENIUS (THE ATTRACTIONS)	*I am attracted to the unfolding and fulfillment of my destiny.*
TIME COMPETENCY (THE SOULFUL CAPACITIES)	*I accept what is, am present to my life, flow with change, and find meaningful patterns in my life.*
WHOLE TIME	*My life is one unfolding project of pattern and meaning.*
TIME MASTERY	*I have all the time I need for life, work, leisure, and more.*
TIME SHIFTING	*I can readily deepen my awareness of the moment.*
EFFECTIVE TIME MANAGEMENT	*My efforts at managing time bring well-being.*
INEFFECTIVE TIME MANAGEMENT	*My efforts at managing time are ineffective.*
TIME STRUGGLE	*I struggle trying to manage my time.*
TIME URGENCY	*I am too busy, impatient, or pressed to get things done.*
TIME STARVED	*I never have enough time to do what I want.*
TIME IMPRISONMENT	*My life is a numbing routine or treadmill.*

If you enjoyed this preview to the Quest for Presence collection of books, please make sure to sign up on my website www.PresenceQuest.life for updates. We offer courses and coaching as well.

Acknowledgments

I appreciate the work of various editors and design assistants who helped bring this book and the entire Quest for Presence (QfP) collection to life: Sue Hansen of Duck Sauce Life, Candace Johnson of Change It Up Editing, Sandra Wendel of Write On, Inc., and Gary Rosenberg of The Book Couple. I appreciate input from Art Wimberley, Cynthia Conigliaro, Faith Geiger, Charles Epstein, Heidi Gray, Stephen Kiesling, Bryan Barbeau, Kristie Ellison, and Michele Studer. Special thanks go to over two dozen beta readers and the diligent assistance of Aldrich Chan, Mary Anne Shepard, and Shelby Pittman. More detailed acknowledgments can be found in the five QfP books.

The seven selected readings in the "A Contemplation" exercise are not meant to be exhaustive or representative of the vast array of spiritual and religious texts that treat the subject of time from a philosophical or spiritual perspective. In some cases, I have adapted or shortened the language from the original text but hope to have preserved the core meaning.

Foundation for Inner Peace (1992). A Course in Miracles. Excerpts from ACIM, T-13.IV; T-17.IV. Used with permission. Please visit https://acim.org/

Johnson, C. (2014). *A better life: 100 atheists speak out on joy & meaning in a world without god.* Cosmic Teapot, Inc.

The diamond sutra and the sutra of Hui-Neng. (A. F. Price, & W. Mou-lam Trans.). (1993). In J. Kornfield (Ed.), *Teachings of the Buddha* (p. 143). Shambhala Publications.

Ladinsky, D. (1999). The Gift: Poems by Hafiz, the great Sufi master. Penguin.

The Holy Bible: English Standard Version. (2001). Crossway.

The Holy Bible: New International Version. (1984). Grand Rapid.

The Holy Qur'an. (A.Y. Ali, Trans.). (2001). Wordsworth.

About the Author

Joel Bennett, PhD, is President of Organizational Wellness & Learning Systems (OWLS), a consulting firm he founded in 1990 that specializes in evidence-based wellness and e-learning technologies to promote organizational health and employee well-being (www.OrganizationalWellness.com).

Dr. Bennett first delivered stress management programming in 1985, and OWLS programs have since reached close to 250,000 workers across the United States and abroad. He is the primary developer of "Team Awareness" and "Team Resilience," evidence-based, culture of health programs recognized by the U.S. Surgeon General as effective in reducing employee behavioral risks. Team Awareness has been adapted by the National Guard and has been used by municipalities, hospitals, restaurants, electrician training centers, small businesses, Native American tribal governments, and in Italy and South Africa. OWLS continues to consult with organizations across diverse industries. Some well-known U.S. clients and partners have included TGI Fridays, Owens Corning, Aetna, Amtrak, University of Iowa, the American Council of Engineering Companies, City of Fort Worth, and the Appalachian Regional Commission.

He is the author or coauthor of these books: *Time and Intimacy: Toward a New Science of Personal Relationships; Preventing Workplace Substance Abuse: Beyond Drug Testing to Wellness* (with Wayne Lehman); *Heart-Centered Leadership* (with Susan Steinbrecher); *Raw Coping Power: From Stress to Thriving;* and *Your Best Self at Work* (with Ben Dilla).

In 2022, Dr. Bennett received a Lifetime Achievement Award from the National Wellness Institute for his leadership in the field of wellness. He earned his bachelor's degree in Psychology and Philosophy from State University of New York (Purchase) and his MA and PhD in Psychology from University of Texas–Austin.

Dr. Bennett was previously on the Prevention Advisory Board for Magellan Health, the board of the Academy of Management's "Spirituality and Religion Interest Group" and the Board of Directors for the National Wellness Institute. He provides Quest for Presence coaching, training, and retreats, as well as keynote speaking, and continues to train facilitators in team (culture of health) and resilience workshops.

He lives in North Texas with his wife, Jan.

Made in the USA
Monee, IL
15 March 2023